If You Love HONEY

Nature's Connections

By Martha Sullivan

Illustrated by Cathy Morrison

Dawn Publications

To the next generation of beekeepers. — MS
To Kathy Davison Lees, a honey of a friend! — CM

Copyright © 2015 Martha Sullivan
Illustrations copyright © 2015 Cathy Morrison

Back matter contributed by Carol L. Malnor and Martha Sullivan

Library of Congress Cataloging-in-Publication Data

Sullivan, Martha, author.
 If you love honey : nature's connections / by Martha Sullivan ;
illustrated by Cathy Morrison. -- First edition.
     pages cm
 Summary: "Suggesting that "you love honey," this
book traces honey to bees, then to dandelions, then to
ladybugs that eat insect pests on dandelions, and so on, tracing a
natural interactive cycle through many connecting organisms.
An educational chart for children traces links of pollination and
honey-making, while material for teachers and parents offers
further background information."-- Provided by publisher.
Audience: Ages 3-8
Audience: K to grade 3
 ISBN 978-1-58469-533-2 (hardback) -- ISBN 978-1-58469-534-9 (pbk.) 1.
Honey--Juvenile literature. 2. Honeybee--Juvenile literature. I. Morrison,
Cathy, illustrator. II. Title.

SF539.S85 2015
641.3'8--dc23

2014048928

Book design and computer production by Patty Arnold, *Menagerie Design & Publishing*
Manufactured by Regent Publishing Services, Hong Kong
Printed June, 2015, in ShenZhen, Guangdong, China
10 9 8 7 6 5 4 3 2 1
First Edition

DAWN PUBLICATIONS
12402 Bitney Springs Road
Nevada City, CA 95959
530-274-7775
nature@dawnpub.com

If you love honey,
Then you must love honey bees.

Honey bees are honey makers. Inside a hive,
thousands of honey bees store honey in the
tiny compartments or "cells" of honeycomb.
Honey is the food they live on all year long.
Honey bees usually build their hives
in hollow trees or in boxes that
people make for them.

If you love honey bees,
   It's no wonder you love dandelions.

Bees use the nectar from dandelions to make honey.
   They suck it up with long, straw-like tongues. It takes
      a lot of flower visits—around 2 million—to produce
         a single pound of honey!

If you love dandelions,
　　You'd be crazy not to love ladybugs.

Ladybugs eat lots and lots of pesky bugs—aphids and
spider mites—that harm dandelions and other plants.
A single ladybug can eat 50 of these pests a day!

If you love ladybugs,
You're bound to love goldenrod.

Goldenrod is a ladybug 'magnet'! Plant it in your garden and you'll have an army of ladybugs standing by to keep your plants pest-free.

If you love goldenrod,
   You're sure to love butterflies!

As butterflies visit goldenrod blossoms, they spread pollen from one flower to the next. This pollen "delivery", called pollination, is needed by goldenrod blossoms to make the seeds for next year's plants. The seeds, scattered by the wind, will sprout into new goldenrod plants come spring.

If you love butterflies,
You just have to love clover!

Butterflies are very picky about where they lay their eggs. They look for favorite "nursery" plants like clover. Butterflies lay their eggs on the clover, where the eggs grow into clover-eating caterpillars. After lots and lots of eating, each caterpillar forms a chrysalis which then becomes a butterfly.

If you love clover,
It would be silly not to love the soil.

Clover depends on healthy soil full
of nutrients and life to grow. A handful
of good soil holds more living things than
you could count in a lifetime. Most are
too small to see with your eyes but
that earthy smell lets you know
they're there.

If you love the soil,
Then you naturally
love earthworms.

Earthworms help keep
the soil healthy. Crawling
through the earth in search of
yummy, rotting things to eat, they
create tunnels and leave behind lots
of nutritious worm poop that
helps plants grow.

If you love earthworms,
It's no accident you love mushrooms.

Mushrooms help speed up an
earthworm's work. Together they
break down the dead things found
in the soil—leaves, roots, and animal
waste—changing the nutrients
into a form that plants
can use.

If you love mushrooms,
    You'd be nuts not to love oak trees!

Oak trees drop thick blankets of leaves every fall. Mushrooms use these leaves for food, slowly turning them into rich forest soil. The leaves are also hide-outs for salamanders, toads, ladybugs, spiders, and butterflies! Older oak trees also drop lots of acorns. These oak tree seeds are important winter food for squirrels, deer, birds and lots of other forest creatures.

If you love oak trees,
    It's easy to love blue jays.

Blue jays not
only eat acorns, they are also 'acorn planters.'
In the fall they collect acorns in a special
sac beneath their tongue and bury them,
storing them for winter food. Although
the jays eat many of them, many others
will sprout and become new trees.

If you love blue jays,
It's a fair bet you love blackberries.

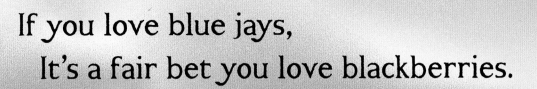

The sweet berries of
blackberry vines give blue jays the
energy to fly. In summer blue jays eat the
berries and poop out the seeds, allowing
new blackberry vines to grow across
the land.

If you love blackberries,
    You can't help but love honey bees!

When honey bees visit blackberry
flowers to collect nectar, they carry
pollen from blossom to blossom.
The pollinated flowers
turn into sweet, juicy
blackberries. In fact,
about one third of the
food we eat is made
possible by honey bee
pollination.

And if you love honey bees,
Then of course you love honey ~ and we
know who to thank for that!

SWEET CONNECTIONS

Can you find the plants and animals in the meadow?

Bees spread pollen so more flowers will grow.

Dandelions hold nectar and pollen for bees and butterflies.

Ladybugs eat bugs that hurt plants.

Goldenrod gives ladybugs a home and holds nectar for bees and butterflies.

Butterflies spread pollen so more flowers will grow.

Clover gives caterpillars a home and holds nectar for bees and butterflies.

Soil and soil critters help plants grow.

Earthworms help make healthy soil. Worm poop is full of nutrients that keep the soil fertile.

Mushrooms are decomposers that change dead plants into nutrients.

Oak trees provide food and homes to many animals. Their dead leaves help improve the soil.

Blue jays spread seeds so more trees and blackberries will grow.

Blackberry flowers hold nectar for bees and butterflies and the berries are food for animals.

From Nectar to Honey

Bees search for flowers that contain nectar. One bee will visit about 100 flowers every time she leaves the hive to gather nectar.

Bees use their long tongues to suck up nectar from inside the flowers. When their "honey crop" in the abdomen — not a stomach but more like a chipmunk's cheeks — is full, they fly back to the hive.

When a bee has found a good patch of flowers she tells the others how to find it by doing a "waggle dance" back at the hive.

Beekeepers collect honey from the honeycomb for people. They need to leave plenty for the bees to eat.

It would take a bee flying 750 miles and visiting 40,000 flowers to make the teaspoon of honey you spread on your bread.

Inside the hive, nectar is unloaded from the honey crop and stored in honeycomb cells, often with the help of other bees. They then begin to change nectar sugars into honey sugars by adding enzymes with their *proboscis* — their long, hairy tongue.

Bees fan the nectar until it gets thick. Then they seal off the cell with wax. Bees will use this stored honey for food.

Pollinating Flowers

As a bee sips nectar from deep inside the flower, she gets covered in pollen.

When she goes to the next flower, some of the pollen rubs off.

Moving pollen from flower to flower is called *pollination*. Most plants can't make more seeds or grow fruits unless they are pollinated.

Bees also collect pollen and take it back to the hive. Both honey and pollen are important foods for bees.

IT ALL STARTED WITH MY BEES

It's easy to love honey bees, or at least the fruits of their efforts—apples, peaches, blueberries, cherries, watermelon, and honey. But when I became a beekeeper, that love grew to new proportions. The hum of a thriving hive, the beauty of perfectly symmetrical honey comb, and the return at dusk of clouds of honey bees on a warm summer's eve—these are the things that I grew to love when I got my first hive.

My love of honey bees soon extended to the nectar-providing plants that kept my bees humming. Plants that I had once looked upon as weeds—dandelions, clover and goldenrod—were now revered as hardy, native, nectar-providers. To help these nectar sources thrive, I tended the compost pile, making sure that the conditions were optimal for the fungi, bacteria, soldier fly larvae and other decomposers that would turn my lawn and kitchen waste into the rich, black compost that would feed my plants.

My plants needed reseeding too, so I invited butterflies, birds and other pollen and seed spreaders into my garden, providing them with the water, food sources, and nesting sites that would encourage them to stay. To help keep my garden pest-free, I welcomed ladybugs, lacewings and other beneficial insects, providing them with bug hotels and a pesticide-free environment that would keep them feasting upon my garden pests for years to come. That's when I realized that I was no longer just a beekeeper. Because of nature's infinite connections, I was now a budding botanist, composter, entomologist and birder—and it all started with bees.

A CLOSER LOOK AT SWEET CONNECTIONS

Pollinators

Honey bees collect nectar and pollen to make their food. In the process, they pollinate plants. About one-third of the world's food supply is made possible because of pollination by honey bees. Without bees, many of our favorite foods such as apples, almonds, oranges, and pumpkins would no longer be readily available.

Despite their importance, bee populations worldwide are declining. Habitat loss, pesticides, climate change, and disease are all taking their toll on bees. Creating bee-friendly habitats, free of pesticides and rich in nectar plants and nesting sites, will help to ensure that bees keep humming for generations to come.

Flowering Plants

When you look at a jar of honey, you can almost see the warm glow of the sun shining back at you. The sun is at the beginning of almost every food chain. The sun's energy is used by plants to make food through the process of photosynthesis. The plants grow flowers that contain nectar. Bees collect the nectar to make honey. Because bees are vigorous and untiring workers, they will usually make more honey than the hive needs; and we collect the surplus honey to eat.

Friends of the Soil

When the roots of plants take in water, they're also taking in the nutrients that are important for plant growth and health. If these nutrients are not replaced, over time the soil becomes infertile and can no longer support plant growth. Nature provides an answer to this problem in the form of decomposers. Decomposers are organisms such as mushrooms, molds, and bacteria that return the nutrients in dead plants and animals back to the soil.

Earthworms also help keep the soil healthy for plants. As earthworms plow through the soil searching for dead leaves and other dead matter to eat, they create tunnels. These tunnels make chambers for the water and air that roots need. Worm poop, called castings, is full of nutrients that keep the soil fertile.

Beneficial Insects

While there are many insect pests that destroy crops, there are also many insects that help crops to thrive. These plant "heroes" are known as beneficial insects.  Predator insects, like spiders, ladybugs, wasps, lacewings, soldier beetles, dragonflies, and hoverflies eat garden pests. Honey bees, bumble bees, moths, and butterflies help plants by pollinating flowers.

Seed Spreaders

Once a flower has produced seed, the seed needs to be spread. Some plants rely on water or wind to disperse their seeds. Others burst open to scatter their seeds. Many plants rely on animals to do the spreading. For example, birds and deer eat berries and poop out their seeds. Squirrels, chipmunks, and blue jays bury acorns for winter storage, but they often don't return for all of them. Some will sprout and grow.

BUSY AS A BEE ACTIVITIES

Help children make the connection with these activities and additional activities online. Use the QR code or go to www.dawnpub.com/activities to get complete directions for each of the following activities. Common Core and Next Generation Science Standards are included.

I Bees

There are many plants and animals that help make honey possible. Some are listed on the bottom of "Explore More — for Kids." Brainstorm ways your class could help each of these "honey helpers." Possibilities include planting a flower garden for bees and butterflies, creating "bug hotels" for ladybugs and other beneficial bugs, making a compost pile for the soil, or building bird houses. Choose one or more projects to do in your schoolyard or home garden.

Sweet Connections

Use the QR code or go to the website to download a black and white version of the meadow ecosystem shown on "Explore More — For Kids." Using the book as a reference, have children draw lines to connect all of the parts of the ecosystem and then color the scene. The result will show a web of interactions between the plants and animals in the meadow.

Hurray for Honey

If you love honey, you'll really like *Honey Bee Ambrosia*— a quick and easy treat!

Ingredients for 4-6 servings: 1/4 cup honey, I/2 cup orange juice, 2 tablespoons lemon juice, 4 oranges (sliced), 1 banana (sliced), ¼ cup coconut.

Combine honey with orange and lemon juice. Pour over banana and orange slices. Sprinkle coconut on top.

Dances with Bees

All animals and insects use some form of communication. Honey bees use a "dance" to communicate the location of flower patches. Science Net Links provides complete directions for teaching children how to do their own waggle dance. sciencenetlinks.com/afterschool-resources/dances-bees/

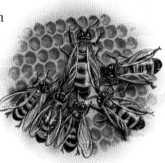

Resources

The Honey Files Teacher's Guide—Video and materials from the National Honey Board. www.honey.com/tools-tips-and-resources/the-honey-files-teachers-guide

The Buzz about Bees: Honey Bee Biology and Behavior— 4-H book. pubs.ext.vt.edu/380/380-070/380-070_pdf.pdf

The Bee Cause: A pack for educators—Games, information, and worksheets from Friends of the Earth. www.foe.co.uk/sites/default/files/downloads/bees_education_booklet.pdf

Tales from the Hive—Videos and information from NOVA. www.pbs.org/wgbh/nova/bees/

Bee Girl empowers communities, including children and farmers, to conserve bees and their habitat. Check out the "Kids and Bees Program." www.beegirl.org.

Educators: There are many wonderful resources online, including activities and lesson plans. Go to www.dawnpub.com and click on "Activities," or scan this code.

MARTHA SULLIVAN is a children's book author with a special interest in nature and sustainability. Born and raised in the US, Martha has also lived in Belgium, Austria, the UK, and most recently, County Clare, Ireland, where she enjoys kayaking, hiking, set-dancing, and gardening. Martha is passionate about her mission—helping children to connect with the natural world so that they are primed to protect it later in life. A Master's thesis on Education for Sustainable Development through the University of Bath was the catalyst that moved Martha from the classroom where she taught Biology for fifteen years to the writer's desk. She now focuses on stories that help children to understand the importance of biodiversity and conservation.

CATHY MORRISON is an award-winning illustrator who lives in Colorado, within view of both the Great Plains and the Rocky Mountains. She watches the plants, the animals, and rain—all close up and personal. She began her career in animation and graphic design, but discovered her passion for children's book illustration while raising her two children. After several years illustrating with traditional media, she now works digitally, which helps the publisher adapt the art into interactive book apps. This is Cathy's third book for Dawn Publications.

Other Books, E-books, and Interactive Book Apps

Pitter and Patter — Ride with two drops over and underground through a watershed — a great adventure.

Over on a Mountain — This recent addition to the "Over" series of habitat books explores 10 mountain ranges, 7 continents, and 20 cool animals. What fun!

In the Trees, Honey Bees — This inside-the-hive view of a wild colony of honey bees offers close-up views of the queen, the cells, even bee eggs. Simple verse engages young children, while sidebars with fascinating information satisfy the older children.

Molly's Organic Farm — An inquisitive and mischievous cat leads readers on a romp through the farm. Discover the interplay of nature that grows wholesome food, from apples to zucchini and everything in between.

Nature's Patchwork Quilt — Nature's many habitats fit together beautifully, just like a patchwork quilt — and each habitat illustrates a key scientific concept.

Noisy Bug Sing-Along — An amazing concert of sounds is happening every day, made by insects that have no vocal chords! **In the book app,** see them moving different body parts to make sounds, then play the matching game.

On One Flower: Butterflies, Ticks, and a Few More Icks — A goldenrod flower is a "minibeast park." Take a close look . . . a butterfly sips nectar . . . a ladybug snacks on aphids. Oh ladybug, look out for the ambushbug! This book is part of the "Mini-Habitat Series" that explores plant-and-animal communities.

The Prairie That Nature Built — Nature in all her glory built the prairie to be full of excitement and beauty, and this new book **and this book app** take children on a vivid journey above, below, and all around.

Mighty Mole and Super Soil — The much-maligned mole may be a pest to some, but this story shows how they are actually mighty helpful.

Dawn Publications is dedicated to inspiring in children a deeper understanding and appreciation for all life on Earth. You can browse through our titles, download resources for teachers, and order at www.dawnpub.com or call 800-545-7475.